Ancient Rome

· · · · · · · · · · · ·

by Alexandra Hanson-Harding

S C H O L A S T I C
PROFESSIONAL BOOKS

New York • Toronto • London • Auckland • Sydney
Mexico City • New Delhi • Hong Kong

DEDICATION
With love and thanks to
Brian, Moses, and Jacob

Cover design by Norma Ortiz
Cover photo by Miwako Ikeda, International Stock
Interior design by Sydney Wright
Interior illustrations by Mona Mark
Poster illustration by Delana Bettoli

Thanks to Magistra Joanne Manse, Latin teacher at Montclair High School,
and Martin Coleman for their help with the Latin.

ISBN 0-439-05920-8

Table of Contents

Introduction

". . . remember, Roman,
To rule the people under law, to establish
The way of peace, to battle down the haughty,
To spare the meek. Our fine arts, these, forever."
—Virgil, Aeneid

Over the course of a thousand years, from 753 BC to AD 476, the Romans rose from being a humble farming people to becoming the conquerors of the Mediterranean world. Their accomplishments in engineering, politics, and the military arts, and their influence on the development of religion changed the world. Their reign was one of the most magnificent times of achievement in world history.

Why should we care today about this long-ago civilization? One reason is to admire and learn from what the Romans were able to achieve. But perhaps more importantly, we should care because Roman civilization has had profound effects on life today. The Roman system of government has influenced the development of governments around the world—including the U.S. It was through Rome's empire that Christianity spread to become the important world religion it is today. And the Roman vision of a world united as one people is one that we still hunger for today.

How to Use This Book

This book has been written to give you lots of ways to help your students learn about Ancient Rome. It combines background information, primary source material, and hands-on activities so your students have a variety of ways to learn about this time period. Although hands-on activities may take time—reading about Roman food is certainly faster and easier than making some—they do make learning more memorable. The closer students are to a real experience, the more likely learning is to stick. Of course, a good activity should be more than just fun. It should have a clear purpose and leave students with a deeper, more meaningful understanding of a concept.

This book also has been designed to let you give your students a feel for Roman life while at the same time helping you meet the five national World History standards. The material and activities give you ways to address the following standards: chronological thinking; historical comprehension; historical analysis and interpretation; historical research capabilities; and historical issues analysis and decision making.

Getting Started

Here are some suggestions about how you can make this book—and the Roman period—come alive for your students

1. Get into a Roman mood

You might want to start by reading a novel about Rome. Robert Graves wrote I, *Claudius* and *Claudius the God* about one of Rome's more thoughtful emperors. These books can also be rented on tape. Colleen McCollough's *The First Man in Rome* is an excellent introduction to the late Roman Republic. Another highly readable book is *Marcus Aurelius*. For fun, you can read the mysteries about Marcus Didius Falco by Lindsey Davis. To get kids in the mood to read more about Rome, they can read *Detectives in Togas* or *Mystery of the Roman Ransom* by Henry Winterfeld.

2. Set the stage

When you begin a unit on Rome, you might want to ham it up. Have the students address you as Magistra (mah-GEE-stra) if you are a woman or Magister (mah-GEE-stair) if you are a man. These words mean "teacher" in Latin. Enter wearing a toga (see instructions on proper toga-wrapping technique on page 56). Cover the walls with real Roman graffiti (for some authentic examples, see page 77). Be sure to display the poster so students can refer to it frequently.

3. Write About It   Talk About It

This book gives you a number of writing and discussion prompts indicated by the logos.

4. Display it

You can use the crafts, games, and activities in this book to help your students create their own Roman "museum" or to hold a "Roman Day." Invite other classes or parents to visit and have students explain their work and share their knowledge. This would also be a good time to perform the read-aloud play on pages 19–22.

Rome Over Time

The Roman Republic

The first Romans were farmers who lived in central Italy. Later, a sophisticated people, the Etruscans, took over and taught the Romans about art, government, and engineering. The Romans learned much from the Etruscans, but eventually they rejected their control. In 509 BC, they kicked out the last Etruscan king and started their own republic.

The Roman Republic survived for hundreds of years, governed, for the most part, by a small group of Rome's most powerful families. But gradually, as Rome got more territory and became richer and more powerful, it became harder to govern. During that time, the aristocratic stranglehold on government was slowly and reluctantly loosened and Rome's poorer people got a little bit more power. But then, Rome was in for a major change again.

In 44 BC, Julius Caesar, a great military leader, had been named dictator for life after a long period of political instability. He hoped to bring much-needed political reforms to Rome. This was a big change for the

Republic, which had generally been run by two consuls for one-year terms, and many Romans were unhappy about it. Caesar was assassinated in 44 BC. After his death, there were more struggles. In AD 27, Julius Caesar's nephew Octavian, who called himself Augustus, became Rome's first emperor.

The Imperial Age

Under the emperors, Rome continued to grow. For the first 200 years, the Roman Empire experienced great stability. This time was called the "Pax Romana" or Roman peace. Rome controlled lands from northern Africa and England to the west and as far as the Persian Gulf in the east. The Romans put their stamp on everything they conquered, from building aqueducts that provided water to constructing sturdy roads for soldiers and trade to building entirely new settlements, some of which still exist as cities today. They brought law and order, too. Many people lived in peace. People could trade across thousands of miles, and people everywhere became richer and more prosperous as less time was devoted to war and self-defense. One Greek philosopher, Aelius Aristides, who lived under Roman rule, said, "As on holiday, the whole civilized world lays down the arms which were its ancient burden, and has turned to adornment and all glad thoughts—with the power to realize them . . . you have accustomed all areas to a settled and orderly way of life."

But Rome had its cruel side as well. Many cultures lost their independence and their own cultural destinies as they became part of the empire and their resources were sent to feed the city of Rome's insatiable demands for luxury goods and crops. Worse yet, millions of people were forced into slavery.

The Slow Decline

For many years, the Roman Empire had strong, effective leaders. The last one was the philosophical emperor Marcus Aurelius. He held on to the empire when it was at its largest point. But eventually, Rome began to rot from within. Its leaders were ineffective. Soon the military, which was once a source of pride, began electing "barracks dictators"—rulers chosen by factions of the army. They were corrupt leaders, but it didn't really matter—one after another, they were assassinated. Rome was facing other problems, too. The barbarians to the north were getting stronger. Rome was getting poorer, and there was an even greater division between the poor and rich. Rome began to spiral downward.

The Emperor Diocletian who ruled from AD 284-305 believed that Rome had become too unruly and big to handle, so he divided it into two empires, the east and the west. Another powerful emperor was Constantine (AD 324). He had a dream that soldiers wearing the Christian symbol on their shields would bring him a great victory. He increased tolerance of Christianity, which began to spread even more widely across the empire. He set up his capital in Constantinople (now Istanbul, Turkey), and eventually became the first Christian emperor. Soon, Christianity spread throughout the empire.

Rome grew weaker and poorer, less able to defend her borders or feed her people. In AD 475, a boy named Romulus Augustulus became emperor. Soon afterwards, German tribes swept down through Rome. He became the last of all the Roman emperors. The Roman Empire was officially over in AD 476, but its influence continues to linger today.

◈ ACTIVITIES ◈

KWL Chart

Students are more motivated to learn if they feel they have a say in what they will learn about. They will also gain a deeper understanding of a topic if they can link new knowledge to prior knowledge. To help activate prior knowledge and give students a choice in what they learn, create a KWL chart like the one below. Create the chart in a place where you can refer to it throughout your unit.

What I Know	What I Want to Know	What I Learned
Rome is in Italy.	How did they get so powerful?	
The Romans were powerful.	What was life like in Ancient Rome?	

Romulus and Remus

The Romans, like many ancient peoples, had a legend that told how their city came into being. Discuss the concept of origin myths with students. Then provide students with a copy of the myth on page 15. After discussing it, encourage them to write a myth about the origin of their town or city.

A Roman Timeline

To give students an overview of Roman history, have them make the timeline on page 16. You may want to create (or ask students to help you create) a larger version of the timeline for a classroom wall. Encourage students to add information to their own timeline and the class timeline as you learn more about Ancient Rome. Invite students to attach drawings and research reports to the appropriate date on the class timeline.

Here are some suggestions about historical periods that students might want to write about:

The first and second Punic Wars
The reforms of the Gracchus brothers
The first triumvirate
The second triumvirate
The reign of the Flavian dynasty
The reign of Trajan
The reign of Marcus Aurelius
The reign of Diocletian
The reign of Constantine

Roman Empire Map

Provide students with a copy of page 17. You'll need to have atlases or globes available to students so they can answer the questions. Students should also compare this map to the poster.

Answer Key: 1. mostly Egypt and Jordan; 2. Turkey, Iran; 3. France; 4. Turkey; 5. Great Britain; 6. mostly Croatia and Bosnia-Herzogovina; 7. Israel; 8. Iraq; 9. mostly Austria and Germany; 10. Spain

Roman Government

The governmental system of Rome changed over time. It eventually evolved into a system of checks and balances. Provide students with copies of page 18. Have students do research in encyclopedias and other resources to fill out the chart that compares the government of the Roman Empire with the U.S. system.

After students have completed the charts, use a Venn diagram to help them understand the similarities and differences between the two systems.

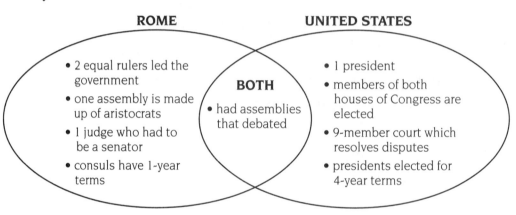

ROME

- 2 equal rulers led the government
- one assembly is made up of aristocrats
- 1 judge who had to be a senator
- consuls have 1-year terms

BOTH

- had assemblies that debated

UNITED STATES

- 1 president
- members of both houses of Congress are elected
- 9-member court which resolves disputes
- presidents elected for 4-year terms

Have students write about their findings. Which system do they prefer? Why?

Read-Aloud Play: Julius Caesar

The reign of Julius Caesar marks the end of the Roman Republic. The read-aloud play (based on Shakespeare's play) found on pages 19–22 is a good introduction to this important figure and important time in Roman history. Provide each student with a copy of the play and assign roles. You may want to the share the information in the box on page 13 with students before they read the play.

Roman Time

According to the Roman calendar there were three kinds of special days each month:

The Kalends—first day of the month

The Nones—fifth or seventh day of the month

The Ides—15th day of March, May, July, or October; or the 13th day of any other month

So Caesar was murdered on the 15th of March, 44 BC.

After students have read the play, encourage discussion by asking the following questions.

1. Who had a better case—Marc Antony or Brutus? Explain your choice.

2. Ask students if they have ever heard of the terms Kaiser and Czar? What languages are they from? What do they mean? Tell them that they both come from Caesar. Why might this term get used for leaders?

Shakespeare's Words

Have students do a reading of Act III of Shakespeare's famous play *Julius Caesar*. In preparation, have them look up unfamiliar words. You might also want to have them read the brief account of the life of Julius Caesar in Plutarch's *Life of Famous Greeks and Romans*. Tell them that Shakespeare's play is based on Plutarch's account.

Have students research how Caesar's grandnephew Octavian became Rome's first emperor. Have them write a classroom play and share it with your class.

Pretend the year is about 40 BC. Have kids divide into two groups of "Senators." Then have them debate Rome's future. Should it be a republic or empire? Have them back up their reasoning.

Genealogy Chart

The first five emperors in Rome's history were descended from Augustus and/or his wife, Livia. Have students use the chart on page 23 to develop an understanding of how they were related to one another. Suggest that students write biographies of any or all of the emperors included on the chart.

Answers Key: 1. Great-grandfather; 2. Claudius; 3. Nero Claudius Drusus; 4. Claudius; 5. Augustus; Caligula

Resources

Books

Julius Caesar, by Michael Grant, M. Evans and Company, 1992

Videos

Julius Caesar, The Shakespeare Plays, BBC/Time Life Films.
Distributor:
Ambrose Video Publishing, Inc.
Suite 1601
381 Park Avenue S.
New York, New York 10016

The Origins of Rome

Romans believed this myth about how their city was founded:

Many years ago, twin boys named Romulus and Remus were taken from their mother's arms and left by the Tiber River to die. But then, a mother wolf found them and took care of them as if they were her own cubs. Later a shepherd found them and raised the two boys himself. When they grew up, the brothers learned they were actually born princes of a nearby town, Alba Longa.

The twins fought to get their kingdom back and succeeded. To celebrate, they decided to build a new city where the wolf had once nurtured them. But the two couldn't decide who should rule the new city, so they fought. Remus was killed and Romulus became king. Rome was named after him.

Now, make up your own myth of how your town or city was founded. **Use gods, goddesses, animals, whatever you want.** *Let your imagination run wild!*

_____

_____

_____

_____

_____

_____

_____

_____

_____

_____

_____

_____

_____

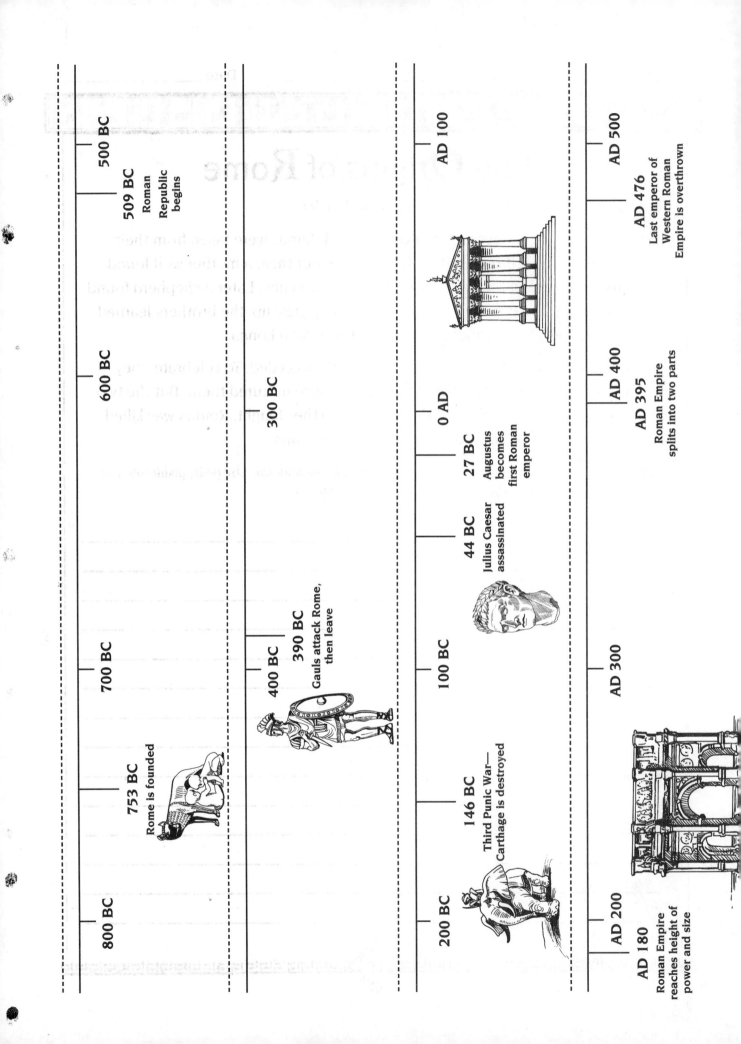

800 BC

700 BC

753 BC
Rome is founded

600 BC

509 BC
Roman
Republic
begins

500 BC

400 BC

390 BC
Gauls attack Rome,
then leave

300 BC

200 BC

146 BC
Third Punic War—
Carthage is destroyed

100 BC

44 BC
Julius Caesar
assassinated

27 BC
Augustus
becomes
first Roman
emperor

0 AD

AD 100

AD 180
Roman Empire
reaches height of
power and size

AD 200

AD 300

AD 395
Roman Empire
splits into two parts

AD 400

AD 476
Last emperor of
Western Roman
Empire is overthrown

AD 500

A Map of the Roman Empire

Can you figure out what countries the following ancient Roman provinces belong to today? Compare the map to a modern map. Then write in the correct answer(s) in the spaces provided:

Regions:

1. Arabia: _____

2. Armenia: _____

3. Aquitania: _____

4. Bithynia-Pontus: _____

5. Britannia: _____

6. Illyricum: _____

7. Judaea: _____

8. Mesopotamia: _____

9. Rhaetia: _____

10. Tarraconensis: _____

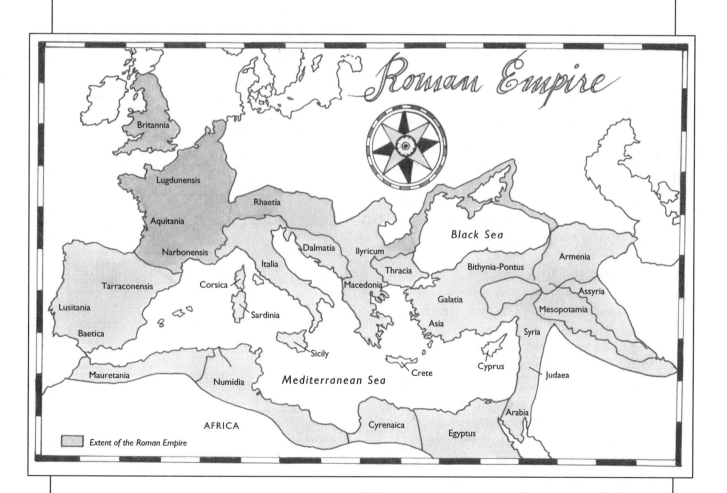

The Government of the Roman Republic

The governmental system of Rome changed over time. Slowly, the government evolved into a system of checks and balances. Have students do research in encyclopedias and other resources to fill out the chart below to see how Rome's government compares to the U.S. government system.

Consuls: These two equal rulers headed the government and, sometimes, led armies into battle. Consuls held office for one-year terms. Each consul's rulings were agreed to be supreme, unless there was a conflict.

U. S. President: _____
_____
_____
_____
_____
_____

The Senate and Comitia: These two assemblies, one of aristocrats, the other of the common people, made the laws. The Senate ran the day-to-day government. It met every working day, held debates, and was especially concerned with foreign policy and money decisions. The Comitia, a people's assembly, was larger but weaker.

Congress: _____
_____
_____
_____
_____
_____

Praetor: This high-level job, which was only open to senators, entailed making sure that Rome's laws are obeyed, and acting as a judge in disputes involving Roman citizens. If one of the consuls is unable to perform his duties, the Praetor steps in as a second consul.

Supreme Court: _____
_____
_____
_____
_____

Julius Caesar

Julius Caesar was a great general and leader. He had big ideas about his place in Rome's history. Caesar thought Rome's political system was corrupt and needed to be changed. And he thought he was the man to bring a centralized government to improve Rome. But to gain the power to make these changes, he had himself declared a dictator for life. This upset many people, especially since it went against Rome's 465-year-old tradition of being a republic. Most upset were a number of Rome's senators, who feared losing their power under a dictator's rule. What would they do?

Characters

Crowd

Cassius, a Roman Senator

Brutus, a Roman Senator

Casca, a Roman Senator

Calpurnia, Julius Caesar's wife

Julius Caesar, famous Roman leader

Slave

Decimus Brutus, a Roman Senator

Marc Antony, a Roman Senator and friend of Caesar

Narrators A-C

✳ SCENE 1 ✳

Narrator A: It is the festival of Lupercalia in February, 44 BC. A great crowd is following Julius. In a side street, Brutus is listening to the crowds and shaking his head.

Crowd: Hail Caesar! Hail Caesar!

Cassius: What's the matter, Brutus? You don't look happy.

Brutus: I've been in a bad mood lately.

Cassius: So you aren't planning to attend the celebration and see the crowds gather around Caesar.

Brutus: I can't get enthusiastic about THAT!

Cassius: So you don't like our friend Julius Caesar?

Brutus: I like him fine. And I know he's a great general who won Gaul for us, but . . .

Cassius: But he is getting too powerful? I agree with you. We are all from great families. Your ancestor Lucius Junius Brutus fought against the last king of Rome so that we would be free of royal powers! We've had a Republic for more than 400 years, and now, it seems as if Caesar wants to become a king himself.

Narrator A: Casca runs in from the festival in the nearby streets.

Casca: Cassius, Cassius! Oh, hello Brutus.

Cassius: You can speak freely in front of our friend Brutus.

Casca: You won't believe what I just saw. Marc Antony offered a crown to Julius Caesar in front of the crowd. Caesar refused it and the crowd cheered. He offered it again—and the crowd cheered when he refused it again. The third time, he refused it again. But I could tell he wanted to keep it.

Brutus: If he keeps this up, he'll undermine our whole way of life!

✳ SCENE 2 ✳

Narrator B: The conspirators meet late at night.

Cassius: If just one of us kills Caesar, he would be considered a murderer, but if all of us do it, we are putting the end to a menace, and we can get the Roman people to agree with us.

Casca: So, here's the plan. On the Ides of March, we wait till a signal is given, and then stab him together. Do you swear to do it?

Brutus: We don't need to make promises—the fact that it's the right thing to do is promise enough.

✳ SCENE 3 ✳

Narrator B: It is the morning of the Ides of March. Julius Caesar's wife speaks to him.

Calpurnia: My love, don't go out. Promise me, you won't go out.

Julius Caesar: What's wrong?

Calpurnia: I had a dream of terrible things happening to you—unspeakable things!

Caesar: Normally, I would think it was just superstition. But so many strange things have been happening recently.

Calpurnia: Yes, remember that man on the street yelling to you "Beware the Ides of March"?

Caesar: Slave, what does the augurer say?

Slave: Oh, sir, something strange happened. The augurer sacrificed a sheep—and didn't find a heart in it!

Calpurnia: All the more reason not to go, my husband.

Narrator B: In comes Decimus Brutus, another senator.

Decimus Brutus: We have a special surprise for you today. So I hope you'll be coming to the Senate House.

Caesar: I promised my wife I would stay at home—she's worried there are too many bad omens.

Brutus: You want me to tell the Senate of Rome that you can't go out because your wife is scared?

Caesar: Well, when you put it that way . . . I can put aside a little foolish superstition. Give me my robe, slave! I'm going!

✳ SCENE 4 ✳

Narrator C: They go to the Senate House.

Caesar: Hello, my friends. How are you today?

Casca: Get him!

Narrator C: They all start stabbing.

Caesar: No! Stop!

Narrator C: Caesar staggers back and forth, and falls down as Brutus plunges the knife into him.

Caesar: You, too, Brutus?

Narrator C: Finally, Caesar dies. Marc Antony enters the room and is horrified.

Marc Antony: What has happened to Caesar? What have you done?

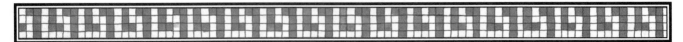

Brutus: We've ended the threat to our Republic. Come to the marketplace and we'll explain why.

Narrator C: He speaks to the other senators.

Brutus: Let's wash our hands in Caesar's blood, and walk out to the Forum shouting "Peace, freedom, and liberty." Then we can let the people know why we have done this deed.

Narrator C: They go out showing their bloody hands. Brutus stands in the marketplace and gives a speech.

Brutus: My fellow Romans, if you want to know why we killed Caesar, here's why: Not that I loved Caesar less, but that I loved Rome more. Would you rather have Caesar live and make you all slaves—or have Caesar die and let you all live free? Right now you are Roman citizens—not subjects of a king. I don't think you want to be ruled by one man. Am I right? If you think I've done wrong, I will kill myself.

Crowd: Live, Brutus! Live!

Narrator C: Then Marc Antony, Caesar's friend gives a speech:

Marc Antony: Friends, Romans, and countrymen. Brutus may be right about Caesar. Brutus is an honorable man, after all. But who filled up the treasury with money? Caesar. And who refused the crown three times when I tried to give it to him? Caesar. And who was it that you all claimed to love such a short time ago, cheering his name in the streets? Again, it was Caesar. Are you not sad now that he is dead? Is there anyone who can take the place of Caesar? Who brought us so much territory? Who was so brave a leader? He was one of the greatest Romans ever—and now he's gone.

Narrator C: The people start to remember what they liked about Caesar.

Crowd member 1: Oh, Caesar!

Crowd member 2: Kill the Senators!

Crowd member 3: Burn them! They have murdered our Caesar!

Epilogue: Soon there is a war between Caesar's enemies, including Brutus, and Caesar's friends, Marc Antony and Caesar's great-nephew, Octavian. But Caesar's death finally ends the age of the Roman Republic. Octavian—who was renamed Augustus Caesar—later became Rome's first emperor.

Emperors' Genealogy Chart

The first five emperors in Rome's history were descended from Augustus and/or his wife, Livia. Study the chart to understand how they were related to each other. Then answer the questions below.

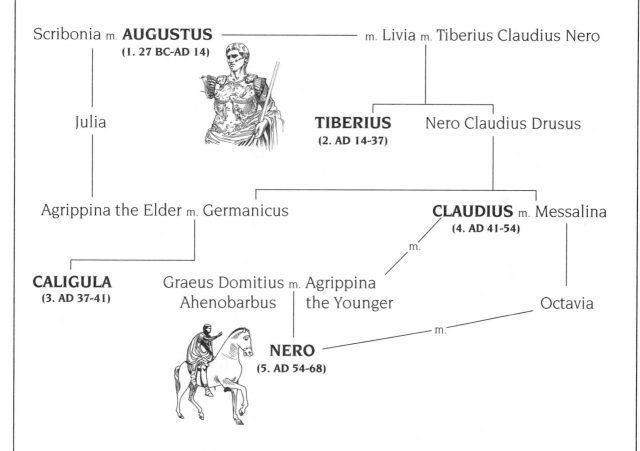

Scribonia m. **AUGUSTUS** ——————————— m. Livia m. Tiberius Claudius Nero
(1. 27 BC–AD 14)

Julia

TIBERIUS Nero Claudius Drusus
(2. AD 14–37)

Agrippina the Elder m. Germanicus

CLAUDIUS m. Messalina
(4. AD 41–54)

m.

CALIGULA
(3. AD 37–41)

Graeus Domitius m. Agrippina
Ahenobarbus   the Younger

Octavia

m.

NERO
(5. AD 54–68)

1. How is Augustus related to Caligula? _____

2. Who ruled after Caligula? _____

3. Who was the brother of Tiberius? _____

4. Which emperor married his niece? _____

5. Which emperor ruled longest? _____

   Shortest? _____

Roman Society

Patricians

Roman society was clearly divided into social classes. At the top were aristocratic Romans, called patricians. They had many privileges and lived lives of luxury. They ran the government. But they had many obligations, too. They had to get up early each day to meet with their clients—people of lower status who depended on them for favors and who they could ask favors in return. Among their clients might be former slaves as well as lower ranking politicians who had slaves of their own. Aristocrats could be required to serve in the military or in a governmental position at any moment. Roman men focused on succeeding in public life and steering Rome's destiny. To stay popular with the people, they had to spend a lot of money putting on festivals and games. These games could be ruinously expensive. During the time of the empire, their roles weakened.

Plebians

But life wasn't easy for most Romans, who were called plebeians. As large farms grew in the country staffed by slaves, it became harder for independent farmers to make a living in the country. So, many people crowded into Rome and not all of them could find work. What was life like for them?

Most Romans lived in tiny apartments in huge buildings called insulae (islands) that were three to six stories tall. Insulae were not as comfortable as apartments of today. There was no central heat or running water. Some insulae were poorly made and the threat of fire was constant. But many people were willing to pay the price just to be able to live in Rome.

Slaves

Most of the work of running the Roman Empire fell to slaves. They mined for gold. They taught the young. They did the paperwork. Some wealthy Romans would have hundreds, or even thousands, of slaves, each to serve a certain specific purpose. How did people become slaves? Some were so poor they had no other choice. Others were captured in war. Some slaves were educated. Others were forced to do horrible work.

Romans could at times be kind to their slaves. Many were affectionate with their slaves, and they often freed them. Freed slaves could become Roman citizens. Still, freed slaves owed their former masters loyalty and often became their ex-masters' clients.

But other times, slave masters were harsh. Slaves who rebelled could be branded or forced to wear iron collars with tags. One tag that was found said, "I have escaped from my post. Return me to the barber's shop near the temple of Flora." And slaves who rebelled could be crucified by the side of the road. There was no excuse for the harm that slavery did to the millions of people whose lives and freedom were stolen from them.

Soldiers

Rome's prosperity was built on the vast empire it commanded, and the command of that vast empire was built on its soldiers. The military made new conquests, bringing in territory, goods, and slaves. They built roads, bridges, and aqueducts. And they helped to guarantee law and order in captured provinces.

What was life like for an ordinary soldier? One word: Tough. Roman citizens could be called up to serve for as many as 25 years. Not only that, when men had to be away from their farms and families for years at a time, they sometimes returned to find their farms in ruin and their families in poverty. But military life had its compensations. Soldiers got to see new parts of the world. They had a chance to share in treasures captured in war. And they got to serve the world's most powerful nation.

? Did you know ?

The main food of soldiers was porridge—right up to the beginning of the empire! Once, Julius Caesar's men had to eat beef because there was no porridge left, and they complained.

Build a Roman Mansion

Roman patricians lived luxuriously in huge houses that had every modern convenience, including running water, large marble rooms, a beautiful open courtyard, and pools to catch rainwater with splashing fountains in them. Students can make their own Roman mansion models by following the directions on page 31.

Create an Ancestor Mask

Romans had a strong reverence for their ancestors, and when someone in their family died, a mask was made of his or her face. The masks were then kept in a special cupboard. Directions for students to use to make masks are found on page 32. This activity will take a half an hour per day for about four days.

Make an Insula

Many plebian Romans lived in insulae. Invite students to make their own model insula by following these directions.

Materials

- 3 to 6 shoe boxes
- markers
- clay
- toothpicks
- tape and glue
- extra cardboard
- construction paper
- copies of pages 33–35
- scissors

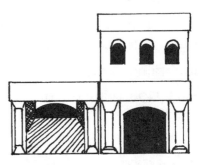

1. Provide students with copies of pages 33–35.

2. Cut off one side of the boxes.

3. Have students cut out, color, and glue the illustrations on page 34–35 to the inside and outside of the shoe boxes.

4. Show students how to stack the boxes up to six layers high.

5. Encourage students to add other hand-made items to their insula.

After seeing these two kinds of housing (mansions and insulae), what have you learned about Roman life?

Slavery took a a tremendous toll by abusing the rights of millions of human beings. Have students learn more about slavery in Rome by having them write a paragraph that tells how it was like slavery in the U.S., and how it was different. Students may want to find out what they can do to help stop human rights abuses today. Tell them they can contact Amnesty International at: www.amnesty-usa.org or 1-800-AMNESTY or write to: Amnesty International USA, 322 8th Avenue, New York, NY 10001.

"We Want You" Poster

Have kids do research on life in the Roman Empire, then have them make up posters saying: We want you to join the Roman Army! Have them include several reasons about why it would be great to join the army in large print.

Then, in small print on the bottom, have them include some of the disadvantages of military life.

Suggest that students write a letter about why they would want to get out of serving in the Roman army, or they might write a letter from a soldier back home to his wife, or a letter from a son explaining why he wanted to join the army.

Pack It Up

All Roman soldiers had to carry their own packs. Packs contained a three-day supply of food, clothes, a bedroll, a bucket, saw, digging tools, and stakes. Soldiers also had to wear full-body armor and carry an iron helmet and all of their weapons, usually a pair of javelins, a sword, and a leather-covered shield. It was about 90 pounds of weight. Not only that, each legion was expected to march 20 miles a day, then build a fortified camp each night.

To give students a sense of just how tough Roman soldiers were, bring a scale in to class. Have students determine how many of their backpacks it takes to total 90 pounds? Let students see how many they can carry at one time.

Make a Battering Ram

Rome stopped at nothing to conquer foreign cities. When cities tried locking them outside of the city gates, Roman soldiers bashed their way in with bundles of logs reinforced with metal heads. After that, resistance was usually futile. They also used catapults to fling boulders or flaming balls of fire over walls when they were attacking an enemy encampment under siege.

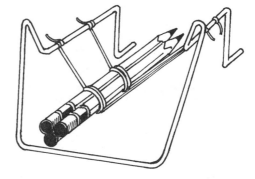

Students can make a battering ram and a catapult following the directions on pages 36 and 37.

Explain to students that a battering ram makes use of the scientific principle (of simple machinery) called momentum. Ask them: Why might this be more effective than using the same piece of wood carried on shoulders? (It's lighter, it doesn't take up that much room, and so on.) After students have completed the catapult, ask: Why did it work? (You may want to explain that as the spoon is pulled back, potential energy is stored; when students let go of the spoon, kinetic energy is released.) How would you feel if you were a Roman soldier using a catapult?

Soldiers Today

Suggest that students find out about soldiers' lives today. Have them read books about soldiers of more recent wars. Ask: How are they different? What are some of the challenges soldiers face today? Suggest that they interview a veteran. Here are some organizations that may be able to help with information.

Veterans of Foreign Wars
406 West 34th Street
Kansas City, MO 64111
(816)756-3390
email: vfw.org/homes.html

Vietnam Veterans of America, Inc.
1224 M Street NW
Washington, DC 20005-5183
(800) VVA-1316
http://www.vva.org

Resources

Books
The Roman Fort, by Peter Connelly, Oxford University Press, 1991

Web Site
For an interesting web site about the history of catapults, check out:
http://www.nzp.com/600roman.html

Roman Mansion

Try to build your own model mansion using a cereal box!

Materials

- green, orange, and blue construction paper
- large, empty cereal box
- white paper
- scissors
- markers
- toothpicks
- tape
- clay

1. Cut a large rectangular hole out of the front of the cereal box, leaving at least 2 inches on each side. This will create the courtyard.

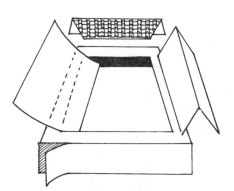

2. Slide green construction paper inside box to make grass. Tape construction paper down.

3. Cut white or beige paper to fit on sides of cereal box. Tape to sides. Then, decorate with markers to look like doorways and arches.

4. Decorate the courtyard by making miniature trees, flower bushes, statues, a pool for collecting rainwater, and so on. You can even make miniature people out of clay.

5. Make a roof for your villa by taking orange construction paper, cutting it to slightly wider than the width left around the cutout rectangle. Fold in half so that roof will be peaked. Using a marker, decorate construction paper so that it looks like a tile roof. Fit it to the top of the box. Cut corners of each piece diagonally so that it will fit close to the piece of "roof" that is next to it. Use toothpicks or tape to affix the roof onto the box.

Make Your Own Ancestor Mask

Follow these directions to make your own ancestor mask.

Materials

- ✣ 1 round balloon for every two students
- ✣ string
- ✣ flour
- ✣ water
- ✣ strips of newspaper
- ✣ tempera paint
- ✣ paintbrushes
- ✣ scissors

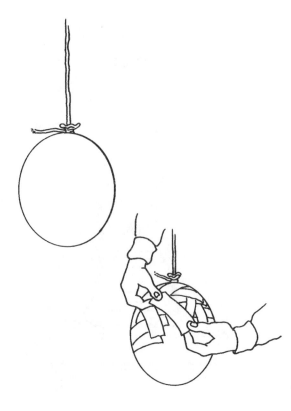

1. Blow up balloon to approximately the size of a human face and tie it. If you have anywhere to let it hang, tie the balloon to the string and let the balloon hang down.

2. Mix flour and water until the resulting liquid is about the consistency of pancake batter. Rip newspaper into strips 1- to 2-inches thick.

3. Dip strips of newspaper in flour mixture and smooth them onto balloon. Do one complete layer per day, letting the strips dry overnight. Repeat process over about three days, until there are at least three layers.

4. When the newspaper-covered balloons are completely dry, take them down and cut them in half lengthwise with scissors (balloon will pop). This will leave you with two face-shaped shells.

5. Paint faces on the shells with tempera paints.

Make an Insula

Here are some things to know about insulae:

✓ The bottom floor was more elegant than the floors above and more likely to have running water. The floors above were more likely to be made up of several apartments (cardboard can be used to make dividers).

✓ Most insulae were ringed with small shops that faced outward on the ground floor. These shops could sell anything from copper bowls to snacks, and were shuttered at night. The shop owners would live in small apartments upstairs from their stores.

✓ Romans decorated their walls with paintings and murals, but didn't have much furniture: mainly beds, small tables, and cabinets to hold their treasures. There were no fireplaces in insulae: most people heated and lit their homes with tiny charcoal-burning stoves.

✓ Most insulae were fairly dark inside because glass for windows was very uncommon.

Materials
✤ shoe boxes
✤ markers
✤ pencils
✤ scissors
✤ clay
✤ construction paper
✤ insulae cut outs

Make an Insula

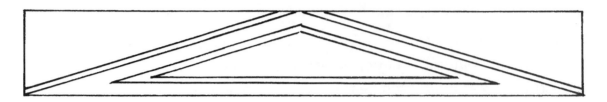

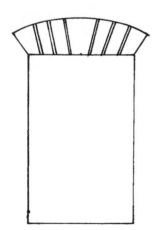 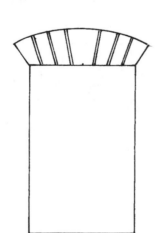 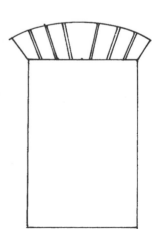

Make an Insula

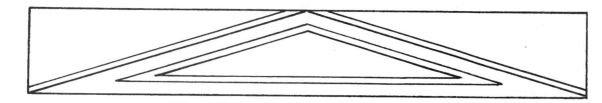

Make a Catapult

You can make your own simple catapult by following the directions below.

Materials
- cereal box
- plastic spoon
- rubber band
- small, wadded-up pieces of paper
- scissors

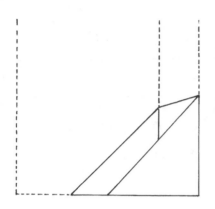

1. Cut off bottom corner of cereal box in a triangle shape that is about three inches at its widest point.

2. In the center of one side, cut a slit wide enough to stick spoon handle into halfway.

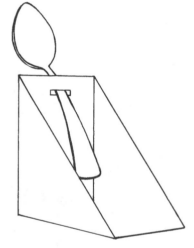

3. Slide spoon handle in, making sure that spoon bowl sticks up above the top of the cereal box.

4. Put rubber band on top of spoon, add wadded-up piece of paper, pull back, and shoot. Watch the paper fly across the room.

NOTE: Only try this with a soft item like paper. This really works—and you don't want to hurt anyone by catapulting a hard object!

A Roman Battering Ram

Here's how you can make your own battering ram.

Materials

✢ coat hanger
✢ string
✢ about six pencils
✢ pliers

1. Untie neck with pliers and bend coat hanger into a shape like this:

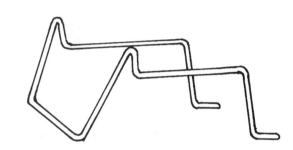

2. Tie bundle of pencils together at two ends, leaving the ends long and even.

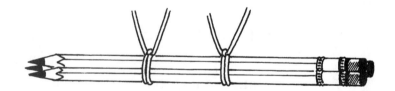

3. Tie the strings to the sides of the coat hangers so that they hang evenly and try swinging the strings forward. Try knocking over a piece of paper.

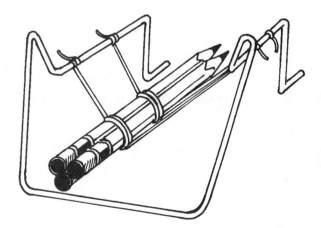

The City of Rome

The Best and Worst of Roman Civilization

A lot of what Rome's city life was like would be familiar to big city dwellers today. Some people lived in mansions, but most people lived in cramped, dangerous high-rises for high rent. The streets were crowded and noisy during the day and at night because night was the only time carts were allowed to go into Rome. The Roman writer Juvenal wrote, "There's death from every open window as you pass along at night . . . . Look at the height of that towering roof from which a pot cracks my head whenever some broken leaking vessel is pitched out of the window . . . you pray in terror that they will do no more than empty their slop-pails over you." To make life even more expensive, it was difficult to cook in the tiny apartments, so people often ate out at taverns and little take-out shops. There was too much unhealthy crowding, fire was a constant threat, and it was dangerous to go out at night.

But in some ways, Romans were very lucky. Because there was little work for poor Roman citizens to do, the government provided them with a certain amount of free food. And they had lots of free entertainment as well, from exciting horse races at the Circus Maximus to gladiator shows at the Colosseum. Even the sights and sounds of the Roman street were exciting and interesting.

The heart of the city was the Roman Forum, a magnificent area of temples and large gleaming marble buildings surrounded by markets. This Roman Forum also had huge arches under which Generals would march in triumphs as they brought back spoils from foreign lands. Rome was a city that showed the best and worst of what Roman civilization had to offer. And even today, much remains of the ancient city to fascinate visitors.

The Pantheon

The Pantheon is one of the most famous buildings of Ancient Rome—and one that is still an attraction today. This special building was designed to house images of the gods. Its present version dates from a reconstruction by Hadrian (AD 120-4). It has a single hole in its roof that lets in light. It also lets in rain, but the dome is so high that the rain normally evaporates before it hits the bottom. The Pantheon is made of horizontal layers of concrete, heavier at the bottom and lighter at the top. Byron called it "severe, austere, sublime."

The Romans were the first to make domes—an incredible engineering feat. Their secrets? First, they understood the principal of the arch. Their second secret was a building material they invented—concrete. The Romans learned how to make strong supports for doorways by using an arch. They cut huge arches out of stone and used them not only for making regular walls but for their huge aqueducts, stone structures that carried water hundreds of miles from mountains into big cities all over the Roman Empire. Many of these structures were so well built that ruins of aqueducts can be found all over the former Roman Empire even today.

Roman Baths

One of the few places Romans could come for relief from the stresses of city life was to Rome's many magnificent public baths. These baths contained not only swimming pools and baths but exercise areas and other facilities for living a good life, including libraries, restaurants, and shops.

First, Romans would go to play sports, then have slaves wipe off the sweat with a curved metal instrument called a strigil. Then they might head for the tepidarium, to take a lukewarm bath. Then, they would go to the hot baths. They might go to the steam room, and then cool off in the frigidarium, a big outdoor swimming pool. They might also play some sports in the palaestra or read books in the attached library. All of this was available to Romans for only pennies a day. It's no wonder that most Romans bathed every single day if they could.

? Did you know ?

Romans actually had running water in bathrooms.

◈ ACTIVITIES ◈

A Map of Rome

Provide each student with a copy of the map of Rome on page 44. Have them answer the questions after they've looked over the map.

Answer Key: 1. Tiber; 2. east; 3. Via Appia; 4. north; 5. Caelian and Palatine

Create a Travel Brochure

Have students look through books and encyclopedias to learn more about the city of Rome in ancient times. Then, have them fold a piece of 8" x 11½" paper into thirds, folding them out so that they are shaped like a travel brochure. (You may want to bring in examples from a travel agency or tourism board.) On the front cover have them write "How to Enjoy Your Stay in Ancient Rome." On the inside, they can use different pages to show what you should see when you're in Rome and why. What should be avoided? What are the dangers? And so on. Encourage students to develop as complete a guide as possible.

Build a Model of the Pantheon

Students can work in small groups to create their own models of the Pantheon and develop a hands-on understanding of arches and domes.

Materials
✤ picture of Pantheon (for model)
✤ water

- flour
- strips of newspaper (1" wide)
- round bowl
- cardboard
- heavy tape
- markers
- small box (like a macaroni and cheese box)
- tape
- glue
- extra paper

1. Have students mix a paste of flour and water until it is the consistency of pancake batter.

2. Tell them to dip the newspaper strips in paste and lay them on top of overturned bowl until covered. After the strips have dried, have them repeat the process.

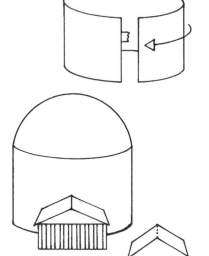

3. Demonstrate how to shape cardboard into a circular wall on which the papier mâché dome can rest. Show students how to securely tape the circle closed. Have them cover it with white paper, and then carefully place the dome on it. Model how to cut the small box into the shape of a portico and attach it to the front.

Build an Arch/Build an Aqueduct

What makes arches so strong—stronger than square door frames—is that they don't just bear the weight of the wall above them, but because of their shape, force the weight down into strong supports. To show students how arches work, try this: Take a long thin stick. Have students bend it. What do they feel?

Encourage students to try making an arch—and, if they want, an aqueduct—with this activity. Again, this works well as a group activity.

Materials

✛ clay   ✛ knife   ✛ small cup   ✛ cake pan

1. Have each group press clay into a cake pan. The clay should be about one-inch thick.

2. Cut the clay into about 12 slices, leaving two slices larger than the others. Take a small cup and push it down in the center of the clay. Leave it there until it is almost dry. Then remove the center pieces and throw out.

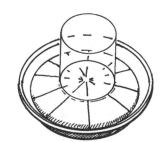

3. Tell students to cut pieces of clay into rectangles that are approximately the size of the pieces in the bowl. These pieces will form the support shafts for the arches. Have students carefully remove half of the circle of clay, keeping the largest piece in the center. That central piece is the keystone. Meanwhile, attach the side triangles (called voissoirs) to the clay support shaft with wet clay. The keystone should go in last.

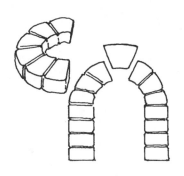

Students can turn their arches into an aqueduct by placing several arches and support shafts in a row.

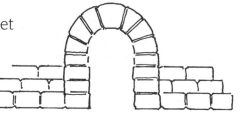

A Diagram of a Roman Bath

Provide students with the diagram of a Roman bathhouse on page 45. Then, have students describe it as if they were explaining it to someone who'd never seen it to tell them how to build it. Write a letter to workmen in a province to tell them how to build one.

Name _____   Date _____

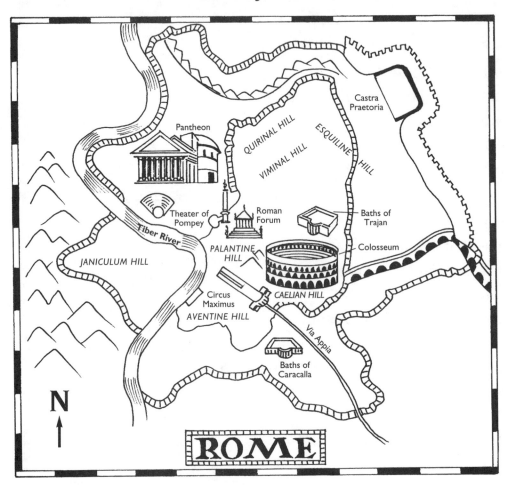

Use the map to answer the following questions.

1. What river flowed through Rome? _____

2. Was most of Rome located east or west of the river? _____

3. Near what road were the Baths of Caracalla located? _____

4. In which direction would you travel if you wanted to go from the Circus Maximus to the Pantheon? _____

5. Between which of Rome's famous hills is the Colosseum located?

_____

Diagram of a Bathhouse

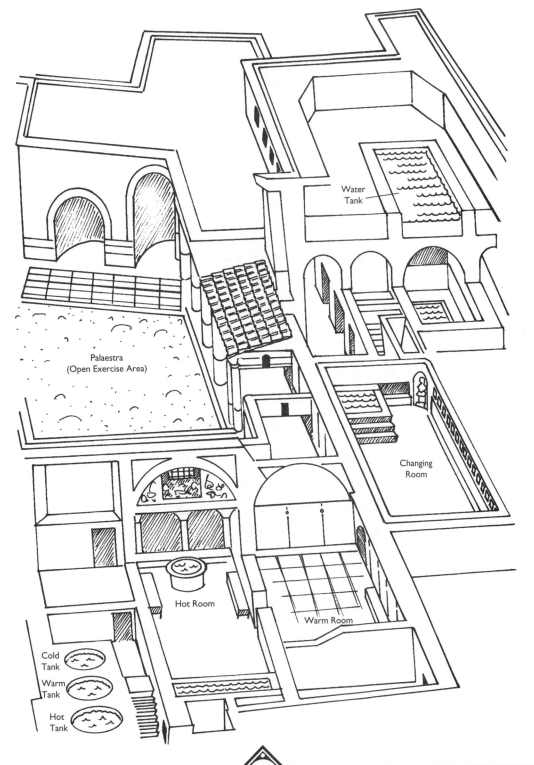

Water Tank

Palaestra
(Open Exercise Area)

Changing Room

Hot Room

Warm Room

Cold Tank

Warm Tank

Hot Tank

Daily Life

Families

In Roman families, the most powerful figure was the paterfamilias—
the father. He had the right to discipline his family, including his wife,
children, and grandchildren and slaves, any way he wanted. He could
even put them to death if they disobeyed him. This practice even held
true for babies. If they were unhealthy or unwanted because they were
girls, the babies would be left on a hillside to die. But as time went
on, the role of the paterfamilias was weakened, and men who treated
their families this way were strongly looked down upon.

In the beginning of the Roman Republic, wives were supposed to be
modest and obedient. Women were passed along to their husbands in
arranged marriages, and a wife was under her husband's complete
control. He could hit her or even put her to death, and her dowry
became his. But later on, women gained the right to control their
property and will it as they wanted. If they got divorced, their dowry
was usually returned to them. Although a woman still needed a male
guardian, she could choose her own. Although women had more
rights than they did in other parts of the ancient world, they could not
hold public office. But many women were very powerful behind the
scenes.

Food

Romans dined in a very different way from the way we do today. Instead of sitting up in chairs, rich Romans reclined on couches in their "triclinium"—dining room. Most dinner parties were very small, only up to nine people, because that is all the people who could fit on the couches. They would eat off a small table in the center with one hand.

Clothing

Everyone wore a tunic: men wore a short one which came to just above the knee, while women wore a long one. But the garment that really defined a Roman citizen was the toga. Wearing a toga well was part of being a Roman gentleman, and men spent a long time arranging the folds of their togas just right. Aristocrats and free-born citizens wore togas. They were shaped like the edge of a circle over two-yards wide and six-yards long along the straight side. Since they were made out of wool, they got warm in the summer. Sometimes, summer togas were made of linen, which was lighter but wrinkled more easily.

Religion

The Romans had an official state religion. They built magnificent temples for Jupiter and other gods. Most of these were borrowed from the Greeks and given new names: Zeus became Jupiter, Hera became Juno, and so on.

The Romans also had household gods called Lares (lar-ays), and gods of the storeroom called Penates that were worshipped with household shrines. Some women who chose to remain unmarried became vestal virgins in honor of Vesta, the goddess of the hearth. For fear of upsetting Vesta, Romans tried never to let the fires go out in their hearths.

The Romans were also deeply superstitious. They believed that their futures could be foretold by the stars and by auguries—mysterious signs that could be interpreted by special priests. Some foretold futures by observing the patterns of birds as they flew, others by watching the ways chickens ate their feed, and others sacrificed animals like sheep and pigs and examined their entrails.

But over time, many Romans began to hunger for a more personal kind of religion. More and more people started worshipping Jesus Christ, even though Christians were severely persecuted under a number of the emperors. In the end, however, Emperor Constantine accepted Christianity and the religion spread across the Roman world. The spread of Christianity became one of the most important legacies of the Romans.

Arts

The arts flourished in Ancient Rome. Many statues, wall paintings, and pottery, often reflecting the influence of the Greeks, still exist today. The work of poets Ovid, Horace, Virgil, and Catullus and of writers like Juvenal and Cicero are still read today.

Holidays, Games, and Entertainment

"Now that no one buys our votes, the public has long since cast off its cares; the people that once bestowed commands, consulships, legions, and all else, now meddles no more and longs eagerly for just two things—bread and circuses," wrote the ancient satirist Juvenal. By the time Rome had become an empire, the mostly poor population of the city was desperate for relief from their cramped, miserable lives. Because most of Rome's work was done by slaves, there were few opportunities for free Romans to find gainful employment. To keep them from rising up against the unfair conditions of their lives, the emperors provided them with an allowance of free grain and with entertainment at public expense during holidays. There were lots of holidays, too. In fact there were so many holidays, that Emperor Marcus Aurelius limited holidays during his reign to 135 per year.

Romans loved cruel spectacles. They forced slaves, criminals, and people whose beliefs they didn't agree with, like Christians, to be killed for their amusement. Huge crowds gathered to watch pairs of gladiators fight to the death. Some victims were forced to fight against wild animals, or were used as human torches. The Colosseum, a famous amphitheater that still exists today in Rome, could even be flooded so that people could be forced to reenact naval battles. Sometimes hundreds of people would be killed in a day, to the general delight of the audience, and the slower and more painful the deaths were, the more the Roman crowds liked it.

Ab Ova Usque ad Mala: From Eggs to Apples

Have students try dining like the Romans did. Get bath towels or blankets so that they can lie on the floor. Have them eat with their hands, leaning on one elbow. For an easy "mini banquet" try serving the following: hard-boiled eggs, olives, figs, nuts, grapes, apples, crusty round loaves of Italian bread, cheese, and grape juice. You might also make and serve the Roman candy described below.

While they are dining, tell them more about the Romans and how they ate. Rich people might eat exotic foods like peacocks, flamingoes, cranes, stuffed dormice, and roasted parrots. But most people had a simple, healthy diet of vegetables and cheese with little meat. They liked mostly fish, poultry, and pork. Beer, milk, and beef were generally considered "barbarian food."

Dulcia Domestica: Roman Candy

Here is simple recipe your students may enjoy making and eating.

Materials

12-16 oz. pitted dates	1 tsp. salt
3 ounces pine nuts (or other nuts)	1/2 cup honey

1. Coarsely grind nuts (try a mortar and pestle, or put nuts between two pieces of wax paper and crush them with a rolling pin).

2. Using fingers or small spoon, stuff pine nuts into the empty holes left behind when dates are pitted.

3. Sprinkle stuffed dates with salt

4. Stew dates in honey on medium-low heat for about 10 minutes, until the outer skin of the date begins to fall away.

5. Wait until dates cool, then serve. Makes about 25-30 dates.

Dress Like a Roman

Students can try making their own togas by following the steps listed on page 56.

 Ask students: What kinds of things denote status in clothing today? Do we have rules, spoken or unspoken, about clothing and the image that it gives us?

Gods and Goddesses Trading Cards

The activity on page 57 will help students gather more information on Roman gods and goddesses.

God's name: _____
Where god came from: _____
Special powers: _____
Special weaknesses: _____
Details (example of their prowess):
_____
_____

Relief Art

Relief sculptures were very popular in Roman times. These sculptures showed everything from battle scenes to scenes of people buying in shops and other aspects of everyday life. They used them to decorate arches and graves. The Romans were experts at making these nearly flat sculptures appear three dimensional. The activity that follows shows how students can create this type of Roman art.

Materials

✤ book of Roman art that shows reliefs for models (or else you can make up your own street or battle scene)

✤ flat slice of clay (should be about ¾" thick, at least about 3" by 4"—size can vary)

✤ toothpicks   ✤ plastic knife

1. Have students draw their design on the clay with a toothpick. If they make a mistake, tell them to just smooth it over with the flat of their knife and do it over until they are satisfied.

2. Tell them to use their toothpick and knife to cut away the background of the picture, leaving the main figures raised.

3. Allow clay to dry, then display.

Mosaics

Romans excelled at the art of making mosaics—creating designs out of small pieces of colored glass. Many beautiful mosaics have been found throughout Rome. One of the most famous was found in the city of Pompeii. It shows a barking dog and includes the warning, *cave canem* (ca-way ca-nem)—"Beware of Dog" in Latin. Students can try making their own mosaic with small pieces of paper and glue. One fun way to make the little pieces is with a paper punch. Encourage them to then make their own designs to fill in.

Still Lifes

Romans painted lots of still lifes in their homes. Some of these still lifes exist today. Students may want to try their hand at painting a still life. Put some fruit in a bowl and suggest that they paint a picture of it. Encourage them to put a border around the painting to make it look more Roman.

The Roman Games

In AD 86, the Emperor Domitian started a new series of games called the Agon Capitolinus. He awarded prizes for sports, poetry, and music. The Agon Capitolinus was modeled loosely on the Greek Olympic games.

Some games you might have your students try are: discus throwing (use a frisbee); foot races, including relay races; and jumping contests.

Stage a Triumph

When Romans conquered an enemy, they would have a triumph—a big parade—and march under one of Rome's magnificent arches. As part of your Roman field day, you can have one, too!

Materials

✛ an arch (can be made of two long sticks, like broom handles, with a cloth banner tied between them, held up by two students).

✛ treasures   ✛ costumes (see page 56)

Cast of Characters:

general   enemy queen   crowd
troops   slaves

Here's the marching order:

—consuls and senators first in white togas trimmed with purple bands

—trumpeters next

—treasures and weapons captured by the enemy held by Roman

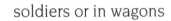

soldiers or in wagons

—animals for sacrifice (most often white oxen with horns painted gold)

—a group of prisoners

—the "triumphator"—the emperor or general who is being honored, wearing a gold and purple robe, riding in a chariot drawn by four horses. In his right hand, he holds a laurel branch. In his left hand, he carries an ivory scepter with an eagle on top. A slave rides in the chariot holding the golden crown of Jupiter and whispering in the triumphator's ear, reminders that he is only a man, not a god.

—bystanders can yell, "Hail Triumphator!"

Gladiators

Rent the movie *Spartacus* (1960), starring Kirk Douglas, and show students the scene where Spartacus is forced to fight in combat with a fellow gladiator. In this scene, two rich Roman couples come to a gladiator school to enjoy a gladiator fight. Spartacus and another gladiator look at each other as they wait to fight. When they battle, the other gladiator is about to stab Spartacus in the throat—and then suddenly tries to attack one of the Romans who ordered them to fight instead. After this, Spartacus is moved to rebel against being a gladiator.

 After showing the movie, ask students to write a letter from Spartacus to his family as he waits to become a gladiator. What would he be thinking? What would he experience as he looked at the other gladiator and heard the noises outside? What would he be feeling?

Extend this lesson by having kids write or talk about if they ever see violence used as entertainment. Ask them to list scenes of violence they have seen on TV, in the movies, or in video games in the past week. What kinds of feelings did watching those things give them? Is watching a violent show on TV or playing a violent video game the same as what the Romans did? Why or why not? Does watching violence lead to acting violently? Should there be less violence on TV, or does it really not matter? What could they do to lessen violence? Is the U.S. a violent society or not? Are we more violent or less violent than the Romans were?

Resources

Books

Food and Feasts in Ancient Rome, by Philip Steele, New Discovery Books, 1994.

Gladiator, by Richard Watkins, Houghton Mifflin Co, 1997.

Make This Model Roman Amphitheatre, an Usborne Cut-Out Models, Usborne Publishing, LTD, 1994.

Toga Wrap

Follow these directions to dress like a Roman.

1. Get a long piece of fabric—15 feet for a 5-foot person, 18 for a 6-foot person, and cut it into a long semi-circle, thin at each end.

2. Let one end of fabric fall forward from left shoulder until it reaches the knee.

3. Wrap other end around waist once, then circle around again until you can bring fabric end over the left shoulder from behind.

4. Tuck remaining fabric neatly into the waistband formed by the first wrapping around the waist.

Create Your Own Trading Cards

The Romans believed in many gods, each of whom had different powers. Below is a list of some of them. Choose some of them—or some of the other gods that Romans worshipped, and create your own trading cards.

Apollo—god of music and light
Ceres—goddess of the harvest
Diana—goddess of the hunt
Janus—god of doorways
Juno—queen of the gods
Jupiter—king of the gods
Mars—god of war

Mercury—messenger of the gods
Minerva—goddess of truth
Neptune—god of the sea
Pluto—god of the underworld
Saturn—god of agriculture
Venus—goddess of love
Vesta—goddess of the hearth

God's name: _____

Where god came from: _____

Special powers: _____

Special weaknesses: _____

Details (example of their prowess):

_____

_____

God's name: _____

Where god came from: _____

Special powers: _____

Special weaknesses: _____

Details (example of their prowess):

_____

_____

Children's Lives in Rome

A Day in a Roman School

From the ages of 7 to 11, boys and girls whose parents could afford it were sent to an elementary school called a *ludum*, run by a litterator or teacher. These schools were often held in marketplaces, and most teachers were Greek. At these *ludi*, children learned to read, write, and do arithmetic. Although the lessons were often boring and repetitive, students took care to pay attention—if they didn't, they could be whipped or beaten!

After the ludum, boys who were lucky went on to grammar school. There, they read Greek and Latin poetry, studied geography, history, and mythology. Most importantly, they studied the art of public speaking. That's because being able to make good speeches was an essential skill for succeeding in public life.

Some young men went on to study at schools that were similar to universities, or even continued their education in Greece, which was famous for its brilliant scholars.

❖ ACTIVITIES ❖

Make a Wax Tablet

Students in ludi learned how to write on wax tablets with pointed sticks called styluses. You can make a wax tablet for your students to try.

Materials

❖ candles

❖ small square or rectangular pan

❖ pot, stove

❖ toothpicks or knitting needle

1. Put 2 candles in a pot over medium heat to melt. Watch carefully! After they are completely melted, pull out wicks and discard. Pour melted wax in a pan and allow to harden completely.

2. Pry hardened wax tablet out of the pan. Allow students to try writing their names or doing one of the Roman math problems (see page 68) on it with a toothpick or a knitting needle.

3. When they are done, students can wipe wax smooth and hand it to the next student. Tell students that for permanent writing the Romans had papyrus scrolls and wrote with octopus ink, but that you don't have an octopus handy!

Latine Loquamur! (Let's Speak Latin)

The Romans spoke Latin. Provide students with copies of page 64 so they can try to speak like a Roman! The reproducibles on pages 65–66 will help them explore the influence Latin has had on our own language.

Latin's Influence

Have students bring in newspapers and select one article from it. Ask them to circle the words with some of the Latin prefixes and roots they explored on pages 65–66. Then have them look the words up in the dictionary. Were they right? Do the words have Latin roots? What do they mean?

Ask kids to find other places Latin is used today. Some places for them to look: on coins, in expressions we use, in medical language, in legal language. List a few commonly used Latin phrases on the board, such as *quid pro quo* and *et cetera*. Have students look up their meanings in the dictionary. Ask students to compile a list of Latin words and phrases and their meanings for a bulletin board display.

 Many state mottoes are in Latin. Ask students: What's our state motto? Is it in Latin? (If not, choose another state with a motto that is.) What does it mean? Then have them write a paragraph explaining the motto.

Making Speeches

Public speaking was a vital part of Roman education and civic life. Have students make their own speeches, choosing a topic of their own or one of the following: Which society has had a greater impact on the world—ancient Rome or the United States? They can use the reproducible on page 67 to help them write their speeches.

Roman Math

Students are probably somewhat familiar with the Roman numeral system. Have them try their hand at Roman math with page 68.

Answer Key: 1. IV; 2. III; 3. XX; 4. X; 5. CM; 6. X; 7. III; 8. XI; 9. D; 10. C

How does our system, the Arabic numeral system, compare with the Roman system? Which is easier?

Studying the Heroes

Children were often exhorted to learn the lessons of brave Romans of long ago days. Some of the real and legendary people students learned about were: Coriolanus; Lucius Junius Brutus; Cincinnatus; Aeneas; Romulus; and Cornelia, mother of the Gracchi.

Ask students: Who are some American heroes whom you learn about in school? How are these Roman heroes like American heroes? What do they say about the values that Americans have/Romans had?

Roman Recess

Now that your students have done hard work during their Roman school day, why not let them try playing games that were played by Roman children? You can set aside a day for them to try a special Roman fun day.

The Romans played a number of board games. Some of them were very similar to games we play today. Although rules may have changed slightly, Roman kids amused themselves by playing games very much like the following: backgammon, ludo, chess, and checkers. Archaeologists have recently found ancient checker boards scratched in the dirt of ancient soil.

Have students follow the directions for three different Roman games on page 69.

Going Nuts

Roman children used nuts in the shell to play games that are very similar to the way marbles are played today. Buy a bag of nuts in the shell and have your students try out this marble game.

1. Using masking tape, make a circle about one foot in diameter on a table. Mark one large nut with a pen or felt-tipped marker.

2. Put two or three nuts in the middle of the circle. Then have students take turns placing their marked nuts on the edge of the circle and rolling or flicking the marked nuts to try to knock other nuts out of the boundary.

3. Whoever knocks the most nuts out wins. Their prize? Nuts, of course! If you want, bring a nutcracker in and let students eat and share their prizes.

Outdoor Games

The Romans had a lot of fun ball games that were described in ancient literature. Here are directions for three different games they played.

Trigon

three players   referee   ball

Rules:

1. Have each of the three players stand about five feet from the others in a triangle. Players toss the ball to each other. As long as they stay in their places and throw to the other players fairly, they can try to trick the other players about whom they're going to throw it to next (referee will judge fair throws).

2. Each player starts with five points. Each time the player fails to catch the ball, he or she loses a point. Whoever is left with points in the end wins.

Roman Ball

An American college student named Wladek Kowalski invented this game based on writings from Ancient Rome. He and many people he's shared it with have enjoyed this fun game.

Draw two concentric circles on the ground, 5 feet and 20 feet in diameter. Players (3 or more) may stand or run anywhere outside the large circle. The ball must bounce in the inner circle, the "strike zone," and pass beyond the outer circle. If the ball is not caught and hits the ground, the thrower gets a point. The player who catches or retrieves the ball throws it next. The first player to reach 21 points wins the game.

Strategy: The player with the ball may run around the circle and try to catch his opponents out of position. The player who catches or retrieves the ball may return to the circle quickly for the same reason.

Etiquette: The first throw can be made by anyone, but should be from standstill. The game then begins on the second throw.

Hoop and Ball

Materials

hula hoop   straight stick

Roll the hula hoop. Chase after it and use your hand or a stick to keep it going. The Romans used a stick with a special notch, but a regular stick will do as well. When you've had a little practice, two or three students can have a race.

Resources

Web Sites

To learn about some more Roman board games, check out this very cool web site:

www.personal.psu/edu/users/w/x/wxk116/roma/rbgames.html

Name _____   Date _____

Talk Like a Roman

You can speak like a Roman! Try these phrases in the Latin language:

Let's speak Latin: Latine Loquamur (la-tee-nay lo-qua-mur)

How do you say it in Latin?: Quomodo dicitur Latine? (kwo-mo-do dee-kee-tur la-tee-nay)

Hello: Ave (ah-way); plural: Avete (ah-weh-tay)

Goodbye: Vale (wall-ay); plural: Valete (wall-eh-tay)

OK: Fiat (fee-ot)

Obviously: Plane (plah-nay)

I don't know: Nescio (nes-kee-oh)

I don't understand: Non satis intellego (non sat-is in-tell-ih-go)

Good morning: Bonum matutinum (bow-num ma-toot-ih-num)

What's your name?: Quid est nomen tibi? (kwid est no-men tee-bee)

My name is _____: Mihi nomen est _____ (mee-hee no-men est)

What's new?: Quid est novus? (kwid est no-wus)

Not much: Nihil multi (nee-heel mul-tee)

How are you?: Quid agis? (kwid ah-gees)

I'm well: Bene valeo (bay-nay wall-ay-o)

Thank you: Gratias (grah-tee-ahs)

You're welcome: Nihil est (nee-heel est)

Please: Quaeso (kwise-oh)

Excuse me: Ignosce mihi (ig-nosk-e mee-hee)

I'm sorry: Me paenitet (may pie-nee-tot)

Tell me: Narra mihi (nahr-a mee-hee)

Is that right?: Verone? (ware-oh-nay?)

No kidding!: Re vera! (ray ware-ah)

Hush!: Tace: (tock-ay); plural: Tacete (tock-eh-tay)

Stop that!: Desiste (day-sis-tay)

Latin Beginnings

We implore (*in*=upon and *ploro*=cry out) you to conspire (*con*=together and *spiro*=breathe) together to investigate (*in*=upon and *vestigo*=follow a footprint) some English words that came from Latin.

According to some estimates, half the words in our language are formed from Latin roots and prefixes. Here is a list of some words that come from Latin. Can you use a dictionary to find out what Latin words they come from and what they mean today? The first one is done for you.

Word	Latin Words:	Meaning:
company	*cum*=with and *panis*=bread	a group of people or friends
abhor		
accumulate		
affluent		
appalls		
calculate		
concoct		
conspire		
derivation		
desperate		
disaster		
extravagant		
instill		
insult		
manufacture		
progressive		
rebellion		
revolution		
senate		
simplicity		

Latin Prefixes

Learn Latin prefixes and they will help you to know more about what the meanings of words might be and whether or not they might come from Latin. Here are some prefixes you should know:

ab—from, away from, down

ad—to

alti—high

ante—before

con—against

de—down, down from, away

di(s)—apart

ex—out, out of

il- or im—not, against

in—in, into

inter—between, among

intro—inward

magni—great

multi—many

ob—against

per—through, complete

post—after

pre—before

pro—for

re—again

sub—under

super- or supra—above

terra—land

trans—over, across, beyond

ultra—beyond

uni—one

What words can you think of that begin with these prefixes? _____

_____

_____

_____

What do those words mean? _____

_____

_____

_____

Make a Speech

In Ancient Rome, young men who went on to higher studies had to learn how to give a good speech. Use this form to prepare a speech of your own.

1. Main point: _____

_____

Three reasons why: _____

_____

_____

_____

2. Second point: _____

_____

Three reasons why: _____

_____

_____

_____

_____

3. Third point: _____

_____

Three reasons why: _____

_____

_____

_____

Now, combine your points into a persuasive argument for your side and present your speech to your classmates.

Do your Roman Math!

Use this chart of Roman numerals to do the math problems below.

1 I	11 XI
2 II	12 XII
3 III	13 XIII
4 IV	14 XIV
5 V	15 XV
6 VI	50 L
7 VII	100 C
8 VIII	500 . . . . .D
9 IX	1000 . . . . .M
10 X	

1. I + III = _____

2. IV - I = _____

3. X + X = _____

4. XV - V = _____

5. M - C = _____

6. VI + IV = _____

7. V - II = _____

8. XV - IIII = _____

9. M - D = _____

10. L + L = _____

Make up more problems to stump your classmates.

_____   _____

_____   _____

_____   _____

Roman Games

Here are directions for three games of chance that were popular with Romans. You can use the score sheet at the bottom of the page for the first two games.

Par impar

In this guessing game, one student hides nuts or coins under a cup. A classmate guesses if there is an odd number or even number of objects under the cup. Change roles and repeat ten times. Whoever makes the most correct guesses wins.

Navia aut capita

Similar to our game of heads or tails. Flip a coin and guess if it is heads or tails. Change roles and repeat ten times. The winner is the person with the most correct guesses.

Micatio

On the count of three, raise some of the fingers of your right hand and have the other player do the same. At the same moment, call out your guess of how many fingers are being held up altogether. Keep repeating until one of you guesses right.

Score Card

Guesses	I	II	III	IV	V	VI	VII	VIII	IX	X
Player I										
Player II										

A Closer Look: Pompeii

Volcanoes

The ancient city of Pompeii was a great place to live in ancient times. The climate was pleasant, the view of Mt. Vesuvius was stunning, and crops grew well in the rich, volcanic soil. But the good life came to an end on August 24, AD 79. That's when Mt. Vesuvius exploded, showering Pompeii's residents with chunks of rock, great heaps of ash, and clouds of deadly gas. When the explosion ended, Pompeii was buried, and thousands of Pompeiians were left dead.

Deadly Mountain

The explosion that buried Pompeii was one of the most intense ever known. Volcanoes are formed when magma (liquid rock) from chambers deep under the ground forces its way out of the earth's surface. Some volcanoes are relatively gentle, like those in Hawaii, which allow thin streams of lava to flow, forming slowly layered shield volcanoes.

Not Mt. Vesuvius. Over the years, a hard crust had formed over the mouth of the volcano, keeping gases in the magma from being released into the air. This allowed pressure to build up in the magma chamber, or the tube going through the mountain to the opening above. So when the magma finally forced its way up to the top of the chamber, the pressure was intense.

When Pompeii exploded, a huge column of gas and pyroclastics (volcanic debris) rose more than 2 miles above the volcano. Soon, a steady shower of rocks, gas, and ash landed in nearby Pompeii. Some people tried to flee Pompeii, but thousands perished. Many were killed by clouds of poison gas. All of those killed were buried under feet of volcanic rocks and ash. Pompeii would lie buried under the ash for more than 1,600 years.

But their devastating loss turned out to be history's gain. In 1748, Pompeii began to be dug up. In 1860, systematic excavations began. What archaeologists have learned from studying Pompeii has taught us about its citizens' agonizing deaths, but has also given us a richness of detail about their lives.

Be a Vulcanologist

The word volcano comes from the Roman god Vulcan, an ancient god of fire. Vulcanologists study volcanoes and try to learn when they are likely to erupt. Vulcanologists still study Mt. Vesuvius. Since the explosion that killed the residents of Pompeii, there have been almost 50 other recorded explosions there. Scientists monitoring Mt. Vesuvius have recorded temperatures in the mouth of the volcano up to 1000 degrees Fahrenheit. So the threat of Vesuvius may still exist today. You can learn more about the science of vulcanology by making a class book or a blackboard display on everything students wanted to know about volcanoes but were afraid to ask. Have students make up diagrams of different types of volcanoes.

Here are some other volcano words for students to research: basalt, caldera, cinder cone volcano, continental plates, crater, earthquakes, geyser, Icelandic volcanoes, lahar, lava, magma, mantle, Pele, pumice, ring of fire, seismometer, shield volcano, Strombolian volcano, tuff, and vent.

pyroclastic flows: Materials formed when magma and rock are shattered by volcanic explosions. They are made up of hot gas, trapped air, and pieces of broken up magma and old volcanic rock and they travel quickly—from 60 to 100 mph.

stratovolcano (composite volcano): Cone constructed by alternating layers of lava and pyroclastic material.

Some students could also be assigned to do research on some major volcanoes. Here are a few: Kilauea, Krakatoa, Mauna Loa, Mt. St. Helens, Paricutin, Pinatubo, Stromboli, and Tambora.

Make a Volcano

Students can follow the directions on page 75 to make their own volcanoes.

Life and Death in Pompeii

A historian named Pliny the Elder witnessed the eruption of Mount Vesuvius in AD 79. He died during the eruption, but his nephew Pliny the Younger later wrote a letter explaining his uncle's experience. Have students read excerpts from the letter on page 76.

 Have students think about Pliny's experience. What do they think of his choices? What would they feel if they experienced what he did? Have they ever seen something dangerous and been tempted to go closer instead of staying away from it?

A Graffiti Wall

People wrote on the whitewashed walls of the Roman world. During archaeological excursions into Pompeii, examples of this graffiti were discovered. Sometimes the graffiti communicated, sometimes it advertised, sometimes it was political. Students can read some real life examples on page 77, and then create their own graffiti wall. Tape a long piece of paper against one wall and have them try writing similar graffiti from things that happened recently.

 What conclusions can students make about Pompeiian life from studying their graffiti? What were politics like? What might the people have been like?

Create a Clay Amphora

The Pompeians and other Romans used amphora for storing food and wine. Provide students with copies of page 78. They can use the ancient technique described there to build their own amphora, just like ones found in Pompeii.

 Write about the last day of Pompeii. Write a good-bye letter or the thoughts of someone at Pompeii. Do research so that you can add as many realistic details as possible.

If a volcano buried your hometown today, and scientists dug it up in the distant future, what would they find? What would their discovery tell them about your life?

Resources

The Romans and Pompeii, by Philip Steele, Zoe Books Limited, 1994
Pompeii, by Peter Connolly, Oxford University Press, 1990
Volcanoes, The Fiery Mountains, by Margaret Poynter, Julian Messner, 1980

Video

Deadly Shadow of Vesuvius, Nova
Tells the story of Pompeii and how it could threaten those who live in the shadow of Vesuvius today.

Web Site

To order or check out lesson plans, take a look at:
http://pbs.bilkent.edu.tr/wgbh/nova

Make a Volcano

Try the following to make your own mini-volcano.

Materials

✤ thin cardboard   ✤ glue   ✤ baking soda

✤ scissors   ✤ tape   ✤ vinegar

Cut out the pattern below and glue it onto a thin piece of cardboard. Then, cut the cardboard into the shape of the pattern and tape it shut so that it forms the shape of a volcano. Take a small paper cup and place it under the volcano. Fill with baking soda. Add vinegar and stand back!

An Eyewitness Account
by Pliny the Younger

On the 24th of August, about one in the afternoon, [Pliny the elder saw]. . . A cloud, from which mountain was uncertain at this distance, was ascending, the form of which I cannot give you a more exact description of than by likening it to that of a pine tree, for it shot up to a great height in the form of a very tall trunk, which spread itself out at the top into a sort of branches . . . [curious, Pliny] ordered a light vessel to be got ready, [so] . . . he ordered the galleys to put to sea, . . . Hastening then to the place from whence others fled with the utmost terror, he steered his course direct to the point of danger . . . He was now so close to the mountain that the cinders, which grew thicker and hotter the nearer he approached, fell into the ships, together with pumice stones, and black pieces of burning rock; they were in danger too not only of being aground by the sudden retreat of the sea, but also from the vast fragments which rolled down from the mountain, and obstructed all the shore. [He went to visit friend at Stabiae, not too far from the volcano. He ate with his friends and went to bed, but in the middle of the night . . .] The court which led to his apartment being now almost filled with ashes and stones, if he had continued there any time longer, it would have been impossible for him to have made his way out. So he was awoke and got up, and went to . . . the rest of his company, who were feeling too anxious to think of going to bed. They consulted together whether it would be most prudent to trust to the houses, which now rocked from side to side . . . or fly to the open fields, where the calcined stones and cinders, though light indeed, yet fell in large showers and threatened destruction. In this choice of dangers they resolved for the fields . . . They went out then, having pillows tied upon their heads with napkins; and this was their whole defense against the storm of stones that fell round them.

[Later] It was now day everywhere else, but there a deeper darkness prevailed than in the thickest night . . . They thought proper to go farther down upon the shore to see if they might safely put out to sea, but found the waves still running extremely high, and boisterous. There my uncle, laying himself down upon a sail cloth . . . fell down dead; suffocated, as I conjecture, by some gross and noxious vapor . . .

Reference
Bullard, F. M., 1968. **Volcanoes**. Austin. University of Texas Press.

Original Graffiti

"For rent, from August 13, with a five year lease on the property of Julia Felix, daughter of Spurius: the elegant Venus baths, streetfront shops and booths, and second story apartments."

"All the fruit sellers with Helvius Vestalis support the election of M. Holconius Priscus as duumvir."

"M. Casellius and L. Albucius are nominated by Statisa and Petronia. May such citizens always be found in the colony."

"This is no place for idlers. On your way, loafer."

"Celadius, glory of the girls, heart-throb of the girls."

"I wonder O wall, that you have not fallen in ruins from supporting the tiresome productions of so many writers."

"For rent from July 1. Streetfront shops with counter space, luxurious second story apartments, and a town house."

"The weaver Successus loves Iris, the slave of the innkeeper's wife. She doesn't think much of him but he tries to make her feel sorry for him."

"I have spoken and written—you love Iris but she doesn't care for you."

"Actius, darling of the people, come back quickly."

"Quintus Petronius Octavius has gained his discharge after 33 fights."

Name _____   Date _____

Make a Clay Amphora

Materials

✛ clay　　　　✛ cardboard　　　　✛ scissors　　　　✛ water

1. Make a disk of clay and flatten it out. Then roll long, thin pieces of clay and make them circle around the clay disk so that it starts to spiral upward. Use a cardboard cutout as your guide.

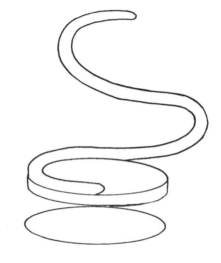

2. When you have built up the sides, smooth them with your fingers. You can wet your fingers with water for an easier time. For best results, make sure the width of the walls of your amphora are even.

3. Add a handle. Allow the amphora to dry.

Summing Up

What's Your RQ? (Roman Quotient)?

What have students learned about the Romans? Let them test their knowledge with the quiz on page 80.

Answer Key: 1. He divided it into two sections; 2. Augustus; 3. Carthage; 4. the arch; 5. Cleopatra; 6. the Etruscans; 7. Constantine; 8. potatoes; 9. the death penalty; 10. palla; 11. Saturn; 12. Mt. Vesuvius; 13. the Gracchus brothers; 14. They thought he wanted to be king; 15. Pliny the Elder; 16. 25; 17. insula; 18. 90 lbs.; 19. public speaking; 20. vestal virgins

 Ask your students to talk or write about some of the following questions about Rome.

—Would you rather live in Ancient Rome or the modern day?

—What do you admire about the Romans? Don't you admire? Why?

—If you lived in the Roman Empire, would you rather live in Rome or its provinces?

—What effects has the Roman Empire had on the modern world?

—What were some of the great accomplishments of the Roman Empire? What have been some of the great accomplishments of the U.S.? How do they compare?

Now that they've finished your unit on Ancient Rome, have students write up a first-person account about life in Rome. Some possibilities include writing about an aristocrat, a commoner, a soldier, a slave, a woman, or an emperor. But, to make it lively, insist that students do additional research and cover some of the following areas:

a. Roman food	c. historical events	e. literature
b. clothing	d. transportation	f. customs

KWL

Look at the KWL chart you and your students made at the beginning of this unit. Point out the questions they had and discuss the answers they found.

Review Quiz

1. How did Diocletian change the Roman Empire?

2. By what name was Octavian Caesar later known?

3. Against which city-state did the Romans fight the Punic War?

4. What Roman architectural innovation helped the Romans build the aqueducts?

5. With which ancient ruler did Julius Caesar fall in love?

6. Which ancient people lived close to the early Romans and provided them with some of their early kings?

7. Which ancient emperor was the first to become Christian?

8. Which of the following foods would Romans not have ever tried: wheat, olive, grapes, or potatoes?

9. What punishment could a paterfamilias give a disobedient son?

10. What was the name of the garment a woman wore that was similar to a toga?

11. Who was the Roman god of agriculture?

12. What was the name of the volcano that exploded and killed the residents of Pompeii?

13. Who were two brothers who were famous Roman social reformers?

14. What did some Roman senators have against Julius Caesar?

15. What Roman historian witnessed the explosion at Pompeii and soon after died?

16. How many years could a Roman citizen be required to serve in the army: 5, 10, 20, or 25?

17. In what kind of building did most people in the city of Rome live?

18. About how much did the packs soldiers carried weigh: 25 lbs., 60 lbs., 90 lbs., or 120 lbs.?

19. What skill was an important focus for students if they wanted to enter public life?

20. Who were the Roman priestesses who tended the sacred flame and were never allowed to marry?